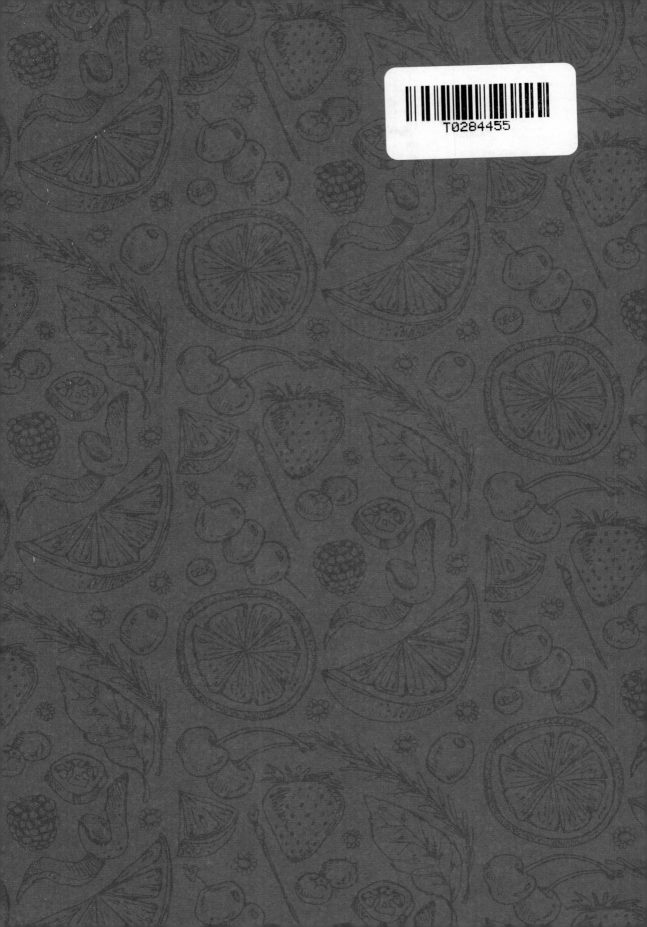

THE BAR(C)ART BOOK

THE BAR(C)ART BOOK

the art of crafting tasty and timeless cocktails

CECE BAILEY PAGE

Other Schiffer Books on Related Subjects:
Mai-Kai: History and Mystery of the Iconic Tiki Restaurant, Tim Glazner, 978-0-7643-5126-6
Seasons Around the Table: Effortless Entertaining with Floral Tablescapes & Seasonal Recipes,
Jessie-Sierra Ross, 978-0-7643-6836-3

Library of Congress Control Number: 2024937869

First printing, 2022
Book cover, book design, and illustrations by Cece Page
Introduction photography by Derek Barker
Author bio photography by Chaise Tinsley
Type set in Mrs. Eaves OT

ISBN: 978-0-7643-6872-1
Printed in China

Published by Schiffer Publishing, Ltd.
4880 Lower Valley Road
Atglen, PA 19310
Phone: (610) 593-1777; Fax: (610) 593-2002
Email: info@schifferbooks.com
Web: www.schifferbooks.com

To my gal pals,
who acted as the catalyst for this book
during that one dinner at DelBar.
You all know who you are.

To Angie and Will,
thank you for such thoughtful editing, feedback, and encouragment.
I'm so grateful for my friendship with both of you.

And lastly, to Sawyer,
you're my favorite person
to make a cocktail for
and always will be.

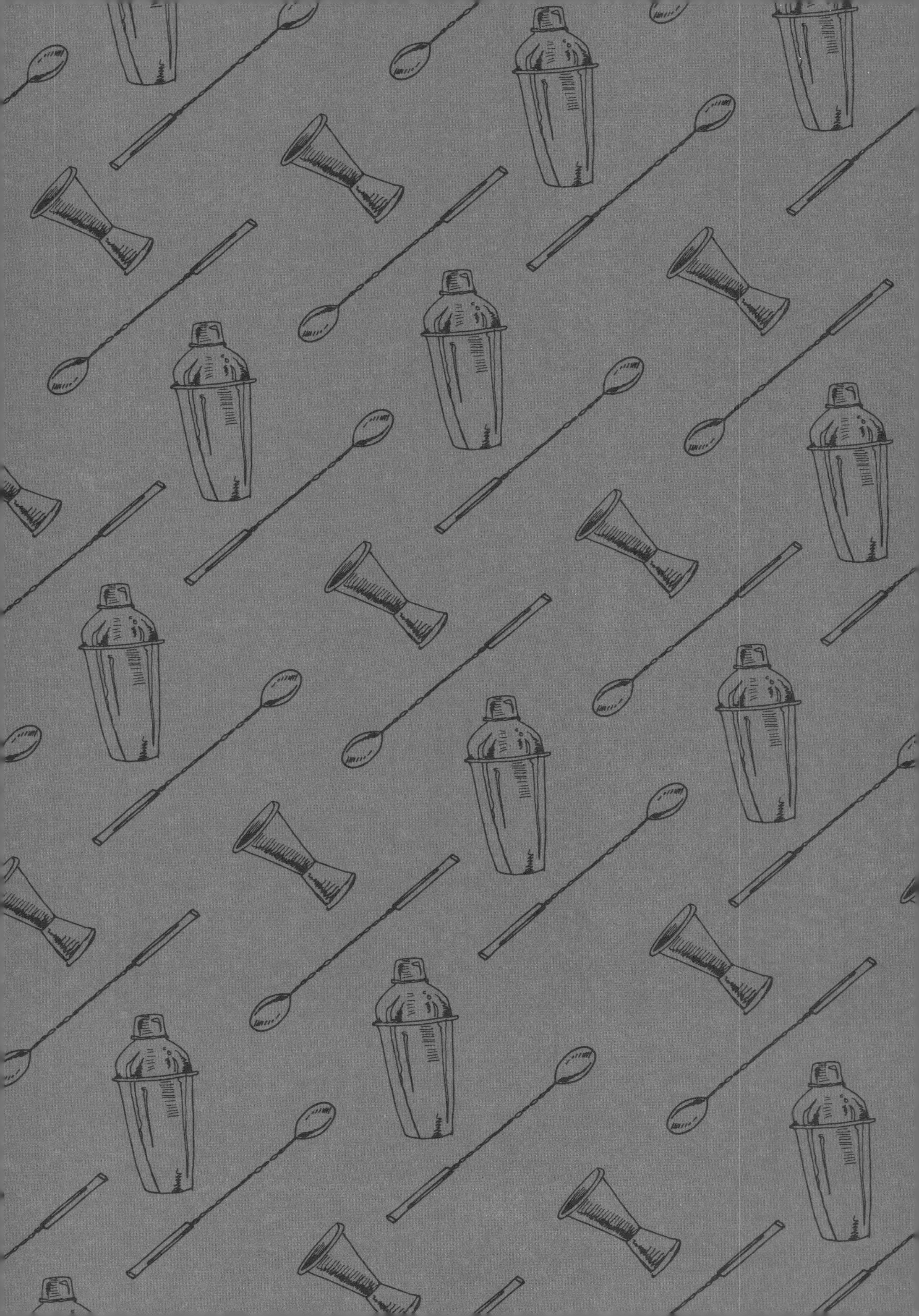

CONTENTS

BAR(C)ART

Before we begin, I should write a disclaimer here: I am no cocktail expert. In fact, I don't consider myself an expert in anything. Instead, I think of myself as an enthusiastic amateur in everything. Especially making cocktails.

I make my living as a graphic designer and artist, but I started mixing drinks as a separate creative outlet after work. My husband gifted me a bar cart and tools, and I soon became the "bartender" at family gatherings and friends' parties. I learned a lot from the cocktail recipe books I received as Christmas and birthday gifts. But I found that many of them were either overwhelming for a beginner bartender or simply too dull to parse through. Making drinks was supposed to be fun, but every time I opened a bar book, it felt like digging through an almanac.

Hence, *The Bar(c)art Book* was born!

I realized that nothing stopped me from combining two things I love: art and cocktails. And with that, why not make it simple, straightforward, and beautiful? So, I decided to pair my illustrations with my favorite cocktail classics and a few recipes of my own. This stuff isn't rocket science, and you don't need a degree in mixology to make drinks. Anyone can read the recipes on the following pages and get started. Poured into this book is a lifetime of passion for thoughtful, thorough, and meaningful art. In this particular case, it's channeled into a medium of booze and bubbles.

The most important thing to remember when you create a cocktail is that it's very similar to a painting; your glass is a blank canvas, and you can paint however you please. There are guidelines and suggestions, but as Pablo Picasso once said, "You must learn the rules like a pro so you can break them like an artist." So remember to have fun with it and create what is beautiful and delicious to you!

Cheers friend,

CECE

BAR TOOLS

Getting started with your own bar might seem intimidating, but you will truly need only a few basic tools. The rest is fluff. The following items are my only must-haves.

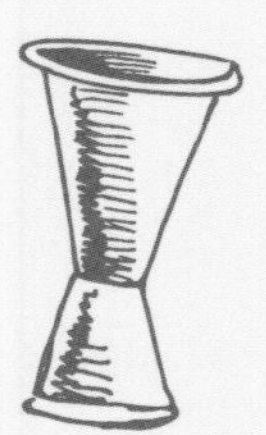

JIGGER

A jigger is your #1 most important cocktail tool. It's an hourglass-shaped measuring tool that is essential for making consistent drinks. The longer end holds either 1.75 oz. or 2 oz. and is used for measuring out your base liquor or mixer. The shorter end is usually either 0.5 oz. or 1 oz. and is often used to measure simple syrup, liqueurs, or secondary mixers.

SHAKER

There are many variations of a shaker, so play around with what kind you prefer. I have a few different shakers, but I make sure they all have a built-in strainer that lets me easily pour my mixture straight into the glass after I've shaken.

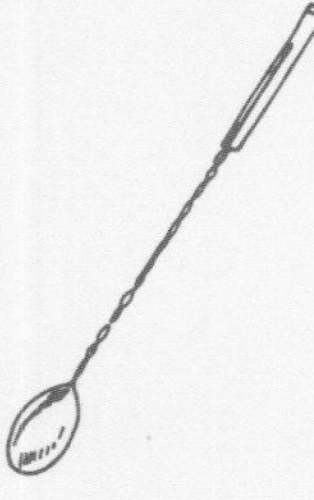

BAR SPOON

A long, skinny spoon that is essential for stirring cocktails you build directly in the serving glass and stir to chill. Think of how you've seen an Old Fashioned being made; stirred, not shaken.

ICE MOLDS

Some cocktails require certain ice to be enjoyed properly. Invest in trays for large ice cubes, spheres, small ice cubes, and crushed ice to take your drinks to the next level.

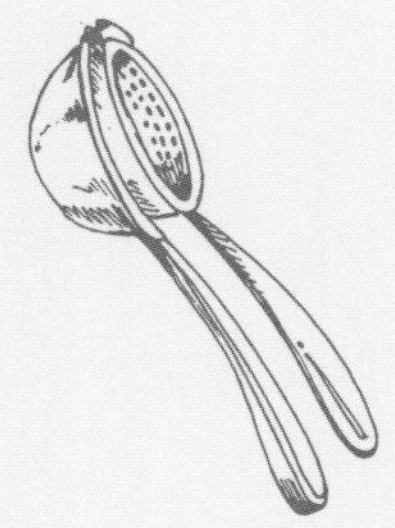

CITRUS JUICER

For me, this is essential. Whenever I mention juice in this book, I'm implying that you squeeze that juice directly from the fruit. The best way to make a good cocktail is to use fresh ingredients whenever possible.

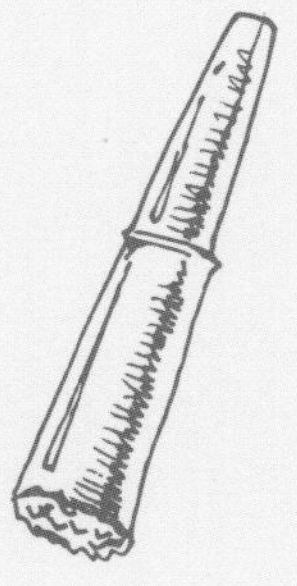

MUDDLER

This device crushes and mixes ingredients in your glass or shaker to express their essence. You'll see ingredients like mint or berries muddled in some of your favorite cocktails. Cocktails like a Mojito rely heavily on this tool, so it's worth the investment.

SWIZZLE STICKS + SKEWERS

These are necessary to me because I view cocktails as a work of art in their own right. Presentation is a huge component of a good cocktail, and collecting beautiful skewers and swizzles to pair with your garnishes will make your drinks all the more memorable.

GLASSWARE

The variety of glassware is endless, but there are just a few variations you really need to make beautiful beverages. Certain glassware can serve a specific purpose to a drink, so it's important to know the goal of your drink before you choose its container.

You can find tons of great, affordable glassware online and in stores, but your local thrift store is the best place to seek out hidden treasures. There are so many old, forgotten cocktail glasses at your neighborhood secondhand shop just waiting to be found. Your drink's vessel is just as important as the ingredients inside. I really encourage you to explore and find pieces that will be unique and make your bar special to you and your guests.

LOWBALL GLASS

Also referred to as the Old Fashioned glass, whiskey glass, or rocks glass. This glass usually has straight sides and a thick bottom to handle drinks that involve muddling. This glass is known for drinks like an Old Fashioned or Negroni but has a universal shape that can be used for most drinks that involve ice.

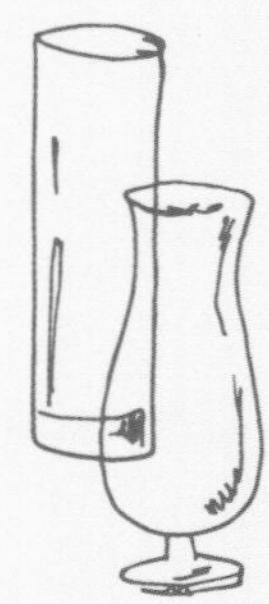

COLLINS GLASS

This glass shape is also called a highball glass, and I use the terms interchangeably. This tall, narrow glass is great for mixed drinks involving lots of ice or beverages with components like ginger beer or champagne; the glass's shape minimizes air exposure and keeps your drink nice and bubbly.

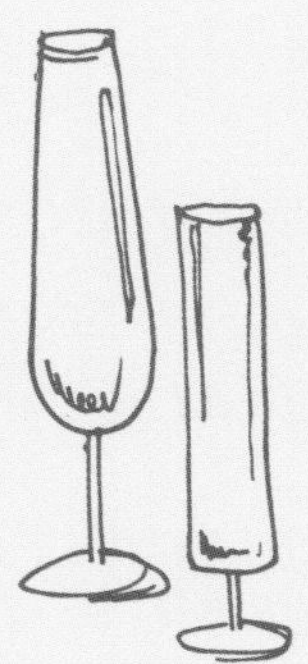

CHAMPAGNE FLUTE

You can use this glass interchangeably with a Collins glass, and it's ideal for any type of drink involving champagne or another bubbly component. Like the Collins, this glass's shape protects the carbonated nature of drinks, but it's a little more elegant if you're hosting an event with an air of formality.

MARTINI GLASS

Also referred to as the cocktail glass. This is the iconic, flared cup with a sleek stem that we all know and love. It's most famously known for housing a Martini, but it can be used with any drink that is served chilled without ice.

COUPE GLASS

The coupe glass, which is sometimes called the saucer, is a wide, bowl-shaped glass that has made a resurgence in recent years. It began as a popular vessel for champagne but is bad at preserving bubbles and, consequently, has grown more popular with drinks like the Last Word, Daiquiris, and other specialty cocktails served without ice.

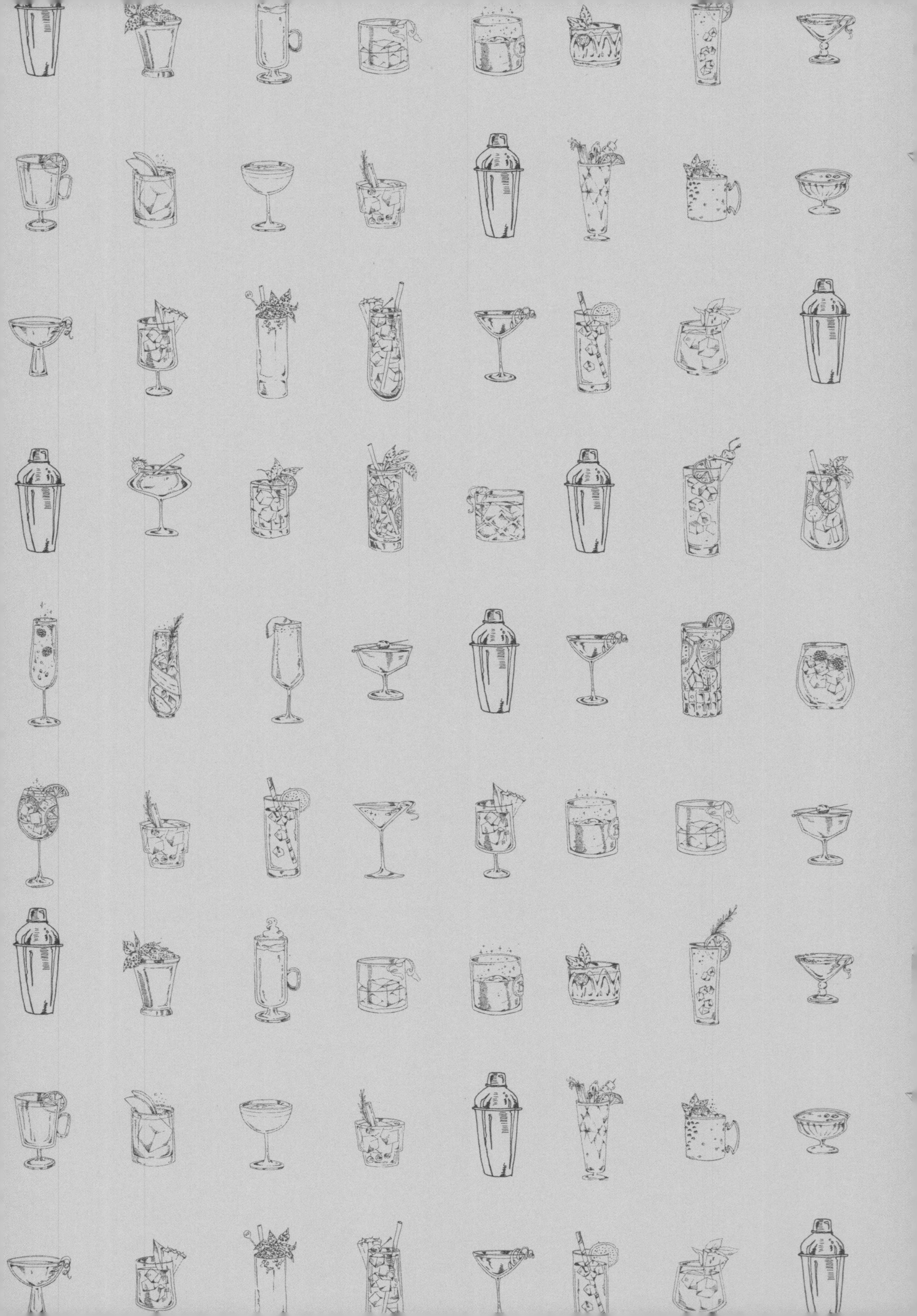

VODKA

All right, it's time for the fun stuff. Let's kick this cocktail book off with good ole vodka.

Vodka is a liquor distilled from rye, potatoes, and wheat. It originated in Russia and is roughly translated from the Russian word voda, which means water. The goal of vodka is to be a neutral, clean flavor. This is why you can easily sip a high-end vodka like Grey Goose, but a cheaper option like Taaka goes down a little rougher (no disrespect; there's a time and place for everything!).

Vodka is an excellent base anytime you aim to build a drink with a prominent flavor profile and want the liquor taste to take a back seat!

LET'S MAKE THE:

Goodbye Earl

SERVES: 4

GLASS: lowball

INGREDIENTS:

6 oz. vodka
2 limes juiced
2 oz. simple syrup
half a jalepeño, chopped
pomegranate juice
ginger beer
mint leaves

INSTRUCTIONS:

Combine all ingredients except the ginger beer and mint in a shaker. Fill with ice and shake until ice cold. Fill 4 glasses with small ice cubes and strain mixture into each. They should each be about halfway full. Finish each drink by filling to the top with ginger beer and adding a fresh sprig of mint.

NOTES:

This drink is not for the faint of heart. I made it with quite the kick, so if you're feelin' weak like Earl, you can skip the jalapeños.

LET'S MAKE THE:

Bonnie Brae

SERVES: 2

GLASS: Collins

INGREDIENTS:

3 oz. vodka
1.5 oz. St. Germain liqueur
2 oz. lemon juice
1.5 oz. rosemary simple syrup
club soda
rosemary sprigs
lemon wheels

INSTRUCTIONS:

Combine the first four ingredients in a shaker with ice and shake until well chilled. Fill both glasses with ice and distribute the mixture evenly between glasses. Top each drink off with club soda and gently stir. Garnish with rosemary and the lemon wheel.

NOTES:

Flavored simple syrups are so easy and very much worth it. To make, combine 1 part water and 1 part sugar. Bring it to a boil on the stovetop, then turn off the heat. Add your flavor, which would be rosemary sprigs, and cover. Let it sit for 15 minutes. Strain into a large mason jar and chill in the fridge. The syrup is good for up to a week.

LET'S MAKE THE:

Moscow Mule

SERVES: 2

GLASS: copper mug

INGREDIENTS:

4 oz. vodka
2 oz. lime juice
ginger beer
lime slices

INSTRUCTIONS:

Fill two copper mugs with crushed ice. Pour 2 oz. of vodka into each. Then add 0.5 oz. of fresh lime juice to each (about 1 lime per drink). Crack open a ginger beer and fill each drink to the top. Garnish with a lime slice.

NOTES:

The Moscow Mule is classified as a "buck" cocktail since it's made with ginger beer and has a "kick." You can swap out your liquor to create different variations. Use bourbon for a Kentucky Buck or your favorite gin for a British Buck.

LET'S MAKE THE:

Espresso Martini

SERVES: 1

GLASS: coupe

INGREDIENTS:

2 oz. vanilla vodka
0.5 oz. espresso or cold brew concentrate
0.5 oz. Kahlúa
0.5 oz. heavy cream
espresso beans

INSTRUCTIONS:

Fill a shaker with the liquid ingredients and ice and shake vigorously. Strain into your chilled glass and gently place the espresso beans on top for garnish.

NOTES:

The secret to the perfect foam is all in the shake. Load your shaker up with more ice than usual and shake longer than you think you need to. This allows the liquid plenty of time to aerate, creating air pockets forming the foam in your drink. I also hold a separate strainer over my glass as I pour the mixture in to further fluff it. Thick and foamy every time.

LET'S MAKE THE:

Bloody Mary

SERVES: 1

GLASS: Collins

INGREDIENTS:

2 oz. vodka
4 oz. tomato juice
0.5 oz. fresh lemon juice
3 dashes hot sauce
3 dashes Worcestershire sauce
lemon wedge
celery stick
olives
bacon

INSTRUCTIONS:

Combine liquid ingredients in a shaker with ice and shake vigorously. Fill a highball glass with ice and strain the mixture in. Add celery, lemon wedges, olives, bacon, and anything else you please to garnish.

NOTES:

This drink has dark beginnings. It's reportedly named after Mary Tudor, Henry VIII's daughter, who became queen of England in 1553 and enjoyed murdering Protestants. Hence, she was nicknamed Bloody Mary. I guess she had so much sass they had to put it in a glass. Enjoy sharing the history behind this drink at your next lighthearted brunch!

LET'S MAKE THE:

Carrie's Cosmo

SERVES: 1

GLASS: martini

INGREDIENTS:

1.5 oz. citrus vodka
1 oz. Cointreau
0.5 oz. lime juice
0.5 oz. cranberry juice
lemon peel

INSTRUCTIONS:

Combine all liquid ingredients in a shaker. Fill with ice and shake until well chilled. Strain drink into your glass and garnish with the lemon peel.

NOTES:

The classic recipe of the infamous drink from everyone's favorite trash television show. For some extra drama and debauchery, sprinkle in edible glitter. As Samantha says, "Hello, my name is fabulous!"

LET'S MAKE THE:

Lemon Drop

SERVES: 1

GLASS: martini

INGREDIENTS:

2 oz. vodka
0.5 oz. triple sec
1 oz. lemon juice
1 oz. simple syrup
granulated sugar
lemon peel

INSTRUCTIONS:

Dip the rim of a martini glass in simple syrup and then sugar. Combine all liquid ingredients in the shaker. Fill with ice and shake until well chilled. Strain into a cold martini glass and garnish with the lemon peel.

NOTES:

This drink can be a chameleon if you want to change it up; for a beautiful lavender concoction, swap the vodka for Empress gin, which comes in an electric purple hue. Going for something more aqua? Swap the triple sec for blue Curaçao.

LET'S MAKE THE:

Cinnamon Toast Crunch

SERVES: 2

GLASS: lowball

INGREDIENTS:

4 oz. vodka
3 oz. Kahlúa
1 oz. simple syrup
2.5 oz. heavy cream
cinnamon stick
cinnamon & sugar

INSTRUCTIONS:

Combine ingredients in a shaker with ice and shake until well chilled. Dip the rims of both glasses in simple syrup and then a mixture that is 1 part sugar to 1 part cinnamon. Place a large spherical ice cube in each glass. Strain your drink into each glass. Sprinkle a dusting of cinnamon across the top of both and garnish with cinnamon sticks.

NOTES:

This is my savory White Russian recipe. And as soon as the calendar strikes December 1, I take the liberty of switching the cinnamon stick garnish out for a mini candy cane. Christmas cocktails? Check.

LET'S MAKE THE:

Cloud Atlas

SERVES: 2

GLASS: Collins

INGREDIENTS:

3 oz. vodka
1 oz. blue Curaçao
1 oz. lemon juice
Sprite
dragonfruit slice

INSTRUCTIONS:

Fill two highballs with crushed ice. Combine vodka, Curaçao, and lemon juice in a shaker with ice and shake well. Distribute half into each glass and then top the drinks with Sprite. Garnish with fresh dragonfruit slices for an extra pop of color.

NOTES:

Just like the novel it's named after, this drink brings together stand-alone ingredients to create a harmonious blend that you can enjoy on any occasion.

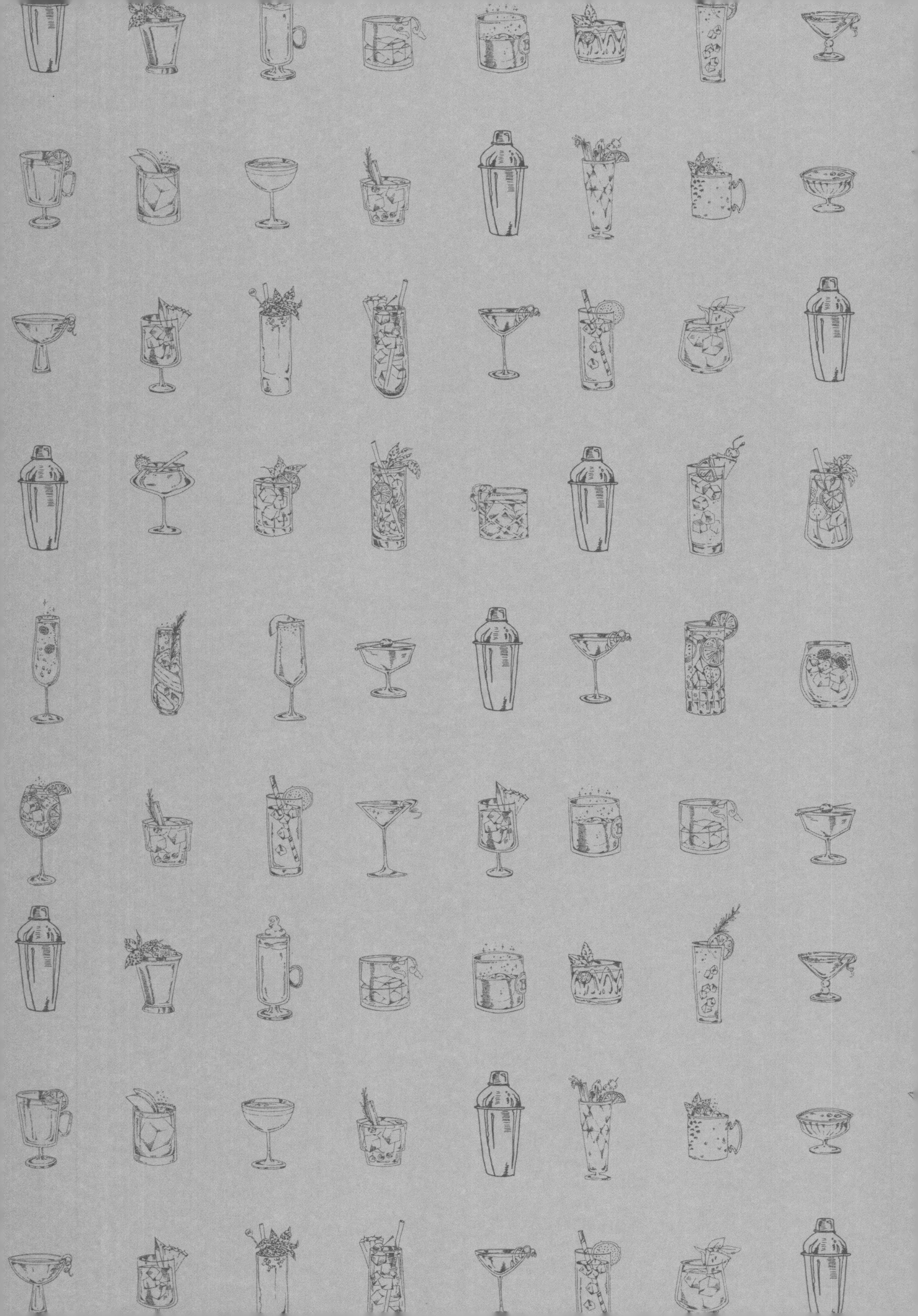

G I N

Like vodka, gin is a clear liquor that is distilled from grain. However, it differs in that vodka is water based, and gin is further distilled using botanicals and juniper flavors.

In fact, the word "gin" is derived directly from the Dutch word *genever*, which means *juniper*. Different gin brands use different combinations of herbal accents, which is why Tanqueray, Hendrick's, Beefeater, and all the others have subtle but distinctly different flavors. Gin is an excellent base for cocktails with fruity and citrusy profiles and is the main component in many famous drinks like a Martini or Negroni.

LET'S MAKE THE:

Dirrrty Martini

SERVES: 1

GLASS: martini

INGREDIENTS:

2 oz. gin
0.5 oz. dry vermouth
1.5 oz. olive brine
olives

INSTRUCTIONS:

Combine ingredients in a shaker with ice and shake vigorously until icy cold. Strain into a martini glass and skewer 3 olives to add as your garnish.

NOTES:

Big shoutout to my sister-in-law, Jeanette, who originally introduced me to this drink and gin. Our favorite tip for this? Chill your martini glass in the freezer beforehand and go the extra mile with blue-cheese-stuffed olives—3 to be exact. Second tip? Roll the Rs as much as possible because I said so.

LET'S MAKE THE:

Watermelon Sugar

SERVES: 2

GLASS: lowball

INGREDIENTS:

4 oz. gin
1 oz. basil simple syrup
4 oz. fresh watermelon purée
2 oz. lime juice
watermelon LaCroix
watermelon wedges

INSTRUCTIONS:

Fill shaker with gin, simple syrup, purée, lime juice, and ice. Shake vigorously and strain into two lowball glasses with large ice cubes. Top each drink with LaCroix and garnish each with a watermelon wedge.

NOTES:

This is a great drink if you're hosting a summer soiree. Chop a watermelon up and throw it in the blender. Except for the LaCroix, multiply everything by 10× and combine in a large pitcher. When it's party time, fill your glasses with ice and add the mixture to each one until halfway full. Top each with LaCroix and use basil leaves as your garnish instead.

LET'S MAKE THE:

Singapore Sling

SERVES: 1

GLASS: Collins

INGREDIENTS:

0.75 oz. gin
2 dashes Angostura bitters
0.5 oz. Cointreau
0.25 oz. maraschino liqueur
2 oz. pineapple juice
1 oz. lime juice
club soda
pineapple or citrus slice
cherry

INSTRUCTIONS:

Add all liquid ingredients except the club soda into a shaker. Add ice and shake well until chilled. Strain into a highball glass filled with ice. Fill to top with club soda and garnish with your fresh fruit.

NOTES:

This classic cocktail was born in Singapore (duh) in 1925. Bartender Ngiam Tong Boon was working at the Raffles Hotel when he noticed that women, who weren't allowed to drink openly at the time, were growing disenchanted with fruit juices and teas. Ngiam was clever enough to craft a pretty pink drink that was both delicious and unsuspecting. What he didn't anticipate was this drink catching on and spreading across the Pacific. Many variations exist, but all feature gin, a cherry brandy flavor, and plenty of fruit garnishes.

LET'S MAKE THE:

Nouveau Negroni

SERVES: 1

GLASS: lowball

INGREDIENTS:

1 oz. gin
0.75 oz. Campari
0.75 sweet vermouth
dry white wine (optional)
orange peel

INSTRUCTIONS:

You will build this cocktail directly in the glass. Start with a lowball glass and place 1–2 large ice cubes. Pour each ingredient in and then stir quickly with a bar spoon to chill your drink. You can add a splash of pinot grigio if this drink is too bitter for your liking. Express an orange peel over the glass and then add as garnish.

NOTES:

The original Negroni was a variation of its predecessor, the Americano, and countless bartenders have created variations of it since. According to legend, Count Camillo Negroni walked into a bar in Florence, Italy, and asked the bartender to make him something stronger than usual. The bartender added gin, swapped the garnish, and voilà!

LET'S MAKE THE:

Last Word

SERVES: 1

GLASS: coupe

INGREDIENTS:

0.75 oz. gin
0.75 oz. lime juice
0.75 oz. maraschino liqueur
0.75 oz. green Chartreuse
brandied cherry

INSTRUCTIONS:

Combine liquid ingredients in a shaker and fill with ice. Shake until well chilled and strain into glass. Skewer a brandied cherry (or two) and add as your garnish.

NOTES:

The Last Word, a cocktail classic originally invented around 1915 in Detroit, is a wonderful, tart drink that you'll love if you grew up a sour candy fanatic. This drink is meant for slow sips, since it is 75% liquor. Savor it.

"The mystery of life isn't a problem to solve, but a reality to experience."

—Frank Herbert, *Dune*

LET'S MAKE THE:

Princess Irulan

SERVES: 2

GLASS: lowball

INGREDIENTS:

4 oz. Empress gin
1 oz. lemon juice
1 oz. St. Germain
sparkling water
lemon wheels
rosemary sprigs

INSTRUCTIONS:

Combine first three ingredients in a shaker with ice and shake until well chilled. Add a large ice cube to two lowball glasses. Strain the mixture evenly between glasses. Fill to the top with sparkling water. Garnish each with rosemary and lemon.

NOTES:

I use Empress gin a lot because the color and smell are dope. I found myself making this particular drink repeatedly on hot days while I'd read on the porch. Hence, it only made sense to name it after the empress in one of my favorite book series. She's observant, elegant, and oh-so-fabulous.

LET'S MAKE THE:

Pimm's Cup

SERVES: 1

GLASS: Collins

INGREDIENTS:

2 oz. Pimm's No. 1
0.5 oz. lemon juice
ginger ale
cucumber slice
mint sprig
strawberry
lemon wheel

INSTRUCTIONS:

Add several ice cubes to a highball glass. Pour in Pimm's No. 1 and lemon juice. Top with ginger ale. Stir several times to chill the drink. Garnish with a long cucumber slice, a mint sprig, a strawberry, and a lemon wheel.

NOTES:

Pimm's is a fruity gin-based liqueur developed by James Pimm in London in 1823. Thank God it made its way across the pond, because this cocktail is so refreshing in the Georgia heat during summer. If you aren't a fan of the ginger flavor, you can swap for lemonade or champagne.

LET'S MAKE THE:

Bee's Knees

SERVES: 1

GLASS: coupe

INGREDIENTS:

2 oz. gin
0.75 oz. lemon juice
0.5 oz. water
0.5 oz. honey
lemon peel

INSTRUCTIONS:

Combine liquid ingredients in a shaker with ice and shake until well chilled. Strain into coupe glass and garnish with lemon peel.

NOTES:

Coupe glasses rose to prominence in France in the 1700s, hitting peak popularity in the 1930s among champagne-sipping ladies. However, their bowl shape made them counterintuitive for holding bubbly drinks, since they maximized oxygen exposure and caused drinks to fall flat quickly. After the champagne flute stole the coupe's thunder, they fell out of popularity. Today, they've made a huge resurgence among noncarbonated cocktails, especially ones like the Bee's Knees, which are aromatic and enjoyable to sniff as you sip!

LET'S MAKE THE:

Jamberry

SERVES: 2

GLASS: lowball

INGREDIENTS:

3 oz. Empress gin
1 oz. simple syrup
0.5 oz. lemon juice
blackberry sparkling water
blackberries

INSTRUCTIONS:

Muddle 2–3 blackberries in the bottom of each glass and then fill with ice. In a shaker, combine gin, simple syrup, and lemon juice with ice and shake until chilled. Strain into glasses and fill to top with blackberry sparkling water. Skewer 3 blackberries and add as garnish.

NOTES:

Surely, we all remember the children's book by this same name? The one where a bear and small child gallivant through various fields, festivals, and faraway lands filled with berries? Yeah, anyways, this drink is an adult-beverage re-creation of that story. Enjoy responsibly.

LET'S MAKE THE:

Gillian's Gin + Tonic

SERVES: 2

GLASS: Collins

INGREDIENTS:

4 oz. gin
1 oz. lime juice
lime wheels
tonic water
raspberries
strawberries
cucumber slices

INSTRUCTIONS:

Place berries and cucumber slices in empty glasses with 0.5 oz. lime juice. Muddle to mix and release essence and flavors. Fill both glasses with ice and then insert additional cucumber and lime slices around the walls of the drink. Pour 2 oz. of gin into each glass and then fill to top with tonic water. Garnish with leftover berries and lime wheels.

NOTES:

This drink is dedicated to my sister, Gillian, whom we also affectionately call Gigi and G-Money. It's her favorite cocktail, but she also reminds me of a Gin & Tonic. G is a breath of fresh air and always timeless. Simply put, G+Ts will never lead you astray, and they're a fun drink to make your own with flavored liqueurs or fruits that you're partial to. This drink will always be a bar cart staple!

TEQUILA

Tequila was born and raised in Mexico, but it has become popular worldwide. It's distilled from the blue agave plant's juice, which grows pretty much everywhere in Mexico. There are several different types of tequila, too, and they each bring a different flavor to the table.

Silver tequila is created and immediately bottled. It's most popular among Margaritas and standard tequila drink recipes. Gold tequila is amber colored as a result of being lightly aged in barrels, and sometimes, additional flavors added or a top-shelf aged tequila mixed into it. Reposado tequilas have been aged between a few months to a year in an oak barrel and usually have a full, vanilla-like flavor. Some people prefer the flavor of reposado to silver in their drinks, especially if they're looking for stronger agave, oak, or vanilla notes. Añejo, or aged tequila, has been put in an oak barrel for at least a year and is usually the smoothest tasting. This type is often sipped straight in a similar fashion to a bourbon.

Lastly, mezcal is a smoky variation of tequila. The blue agave plant is usually roasted for longer before the distillation process, giving it its delicious, smoky flavor. This one's my go-to. I love a good smokeshow. Wink wink.

LET'S MAKE THE:

Cecé's Margarita

SERVES: 2

GLASS: lowball

INGREDIENTS:

4 oz. silver tequila
1 oz. simple syrup
2 oz. lime juice
2 oz. grapefruit juice
margarita salt or Tajín
lime wheels

INSTRUCTIONS:

Combine your ingredients in a shaker with ice and shake vigorously. Rim your glasses with salt or Tajín seasoning and fill with ice. Strain your drink into your glasses and garnish with lime wheels.

NOTES:

This is the drink that started my cocktail journey. I never loved the triple sec or orange juice in traditional Margaritas and found myself experimenting. I had so much fun doing so that I requested a bar cart and tools for Christmas a few years ago. You can turn this recipe into a classic Paloma by transferring it to a highball glass and filling the remainder with Topo Chico or Jarritos soda.

LET'S MAKE THE:

SERVES: 2

GLASS: lowball or Collins

INGREDIENTS:

4 oz. silver tequila
1 oz. simple syrup
3 oz. lime juice
Topo Chico sparkling water
lime wheels

INSTRUCTIONS:

Build this drink directly in each glass. Fill both with ice and then add 2 oz. tequila, 0.5 oz. simple syrup, and 1.5 oz. lime juice in each. Fill each to the top with Topo Chico and stir gently to chill. Garnish with lime. If you prefer, salt your rim before making this drink, for an extra kick.

NOTES:

The Ranch Water is a Texas-style highball drink that is basically a spritzer version of a Margarita. The name supposedly comes from the notion that Texas ranchers preferred this thirst-quenching beverage to actual water after a long workday. Honestly, me too. After a long day in the heat, I can't think of anything that beats this drink.

LET'S MAKE THE:

SERVES:

6-8

GLASS:

lowball

INGREDIENTS:

10 oz. silver tequila
3-4 fresh peaches, frozen
juice of 5 limes
4 oz. simple syrup
1 jalapeño
4-5 ice cubes
Tajín
jalapeño slices
lime wheels

INSTRUCTIONS:

In a blender, combine all ingredients except for Tajín and your garnishes. Blend until smooth. Drizzle lime juice on the side of your glasses and dip in Tajín for a statement rim. Distribute frozen margarita mixture among all the glasses and add jalapeño slices and lime wheels to garnish.

NOTES:

This one came about one weekend at the lake with my husband's family. Georgia summers are unbeatable, and the farmers markets always have the best fresh fruit. My father-in-law, Arnall, brought a ton of peaches from a fruit stand and requested a peach cobbler from me, but everyone else wanted a cocktail. I was without most of my bar tools, so I opted for a frozen drink using the blender. You can downsize this recipe for a solo beverage, but I think it tastes best when you drink it in good company.

LET'S MAKE THE:

Mama Dragon

SERVES: 2

GLASS: lowball

INGREDIENTS:

4 oz. mezcal
4 oz. cranberry juice
1 oz. simple syrup
2 oz. lime juice
fresh cranberries
dehydrated orange wheels
rosemary sprigs

INSTRUCTIONS:

Combine all liquid ingredients in a shaker with ice and shake until well chilled. Strain into your glasses filled with small ice cubes. Garnish with fresh cranberries, orange wheel, and rosemary.

NOTES:

If you know me, you know there has to be a *Shrek* reference somewhere in this book. Well, this is it. This drink is sultry, sassy, and the perfect shade of maroon to match the scales of Donkey's baby mama.

LET'S MAKE THE:

Bang Bang

SERVES: 2

GLASS: coupe

INGREDIENTS:

4 oz. reposado tequila
2 oz. Cointreau
1.5 oz. Aperol
2 oz. grapefruit juice
2.5 oz. lime juice
1/2 jalapeño chopped

INSTRUCTIONS:

Combine all ingredients, including jalapeño, and shake vigorously in a shaker with ice. Strain into two coupe glasses and float a few extra jalapeño slices on top as garnish.

NOTES:

The Bang Bang is full of zest and comes in a nice, vibrant coral hue. At first glance, you might assume this drink is best suited for summer, but it's actually a great option for the colder months; the pepper and reposado combination creates a bold, smoky flavor that keeps you cozy as you sip.

LET'S MAKE THE:

Black Magic

SERVES: 1

GLASS: martini

INGREDIENTS:

1 oz. añejo tequila
1 oz. vodka
2 oz. Kahlúa

INSTRUCTIONS:

Combine all ingredients in a shaker with ice and shake until well chilled. Strain into a chilled glass and serve immediately.

NOTES:

This drink is dramatic and bold and pours in a beautiful ink color. If you want to make it festive for something like Halloween, consider adding an eccentric garnish like rock candy or a candy eyeball.

LET'S MAKE THE:

Smoked Cider

SERVES:

2

GLASS:

lowball

INGREDIENTS:

4 oz. mezcal
2 oz. Cointreau
6 oz. pressed apple cider
2 oz. lime juice
cinnamon
nutmeg
granulated sugar
allspice
dehydrated orange slices

INSTRUCTIONS:

Rim glasses with a mixture of 2 parts sugar, 1 part cinnamon, 1 part allspice. Place 1–2 large ice cubes in each glass. Combine the mezcal, Cointreau, cider, lime juice, and a few dashes of cinnamon and nutmeg in a shaker. Add ice and shake until chilled. Strain into your glasses and garnish with a dehydrated orange slice.

NOTES:

To dehydrate citrus for garnishes, cut your fruit into thin slices. Throw those babies on a baking sheet in the oven. Bake at 200°F for 4-5 hours. You might have to flip them over halfway through. Your house will smell fantastic, and you can use leftovers to make a citrus garland across your mantle or doorway.

LET'S MAKE THE:

Bandaloop

SERVES: 2

GLASS: lowball

INGREDIENTS:

4 oz. mezcal
2 oz. coconut cream
1 oz. simple syrup
2 oz. lime juice
0.5 oz. Cointreau
0.5 oz. Aperol
Tajín

INSTRUCTIONS:

Combine all liquid ingredients in a shaker with ice and shake until well chilled. Rim each cocktail glass with Tajín and fill it with ice. Strain the beverage into each glass and sprinkle Tajín across the top as a garnish.

NOTES:

I based this cocktail on the Bandaloop Doctors in Tom Robbins's book *Jitterbug Perfume*. They are masters of immortality and keep things spunky and sultry. Their secret to a longer life? Just follow your bliss. So I'll take that as a cue to get lost in the sauce of this creamy coconut concoction. Cheers!

LET'S MAKE THE:

La Conga

SERVES: 2

GLASS: Collins

INGREDIENTS:

4 oz. silver tequila
2 oz. pineapple juice
3 dashes Angostura bitters
club soda
lemon wheels

INSTRUCTIONS:

You will build this drink directly in the glass. Fill both with ice and start by saturating the cubes with bitters. Next, add the tequila and pineapple juice. Stir gently with your bar spoon to chill. Fill each to the top with club soda and garnish with a lemon wheel.

NOTES:

The unexpected pairing of pineapple juice and bitters creates a complex drink that tastes tropical and earthy. You can dress this up as a "summer bevvy" with a pineapple slice garnish or give it a holiday vibe by embellishing it with a dehydrated orange wheel and brandied cherry. Get you a girl who can do both.

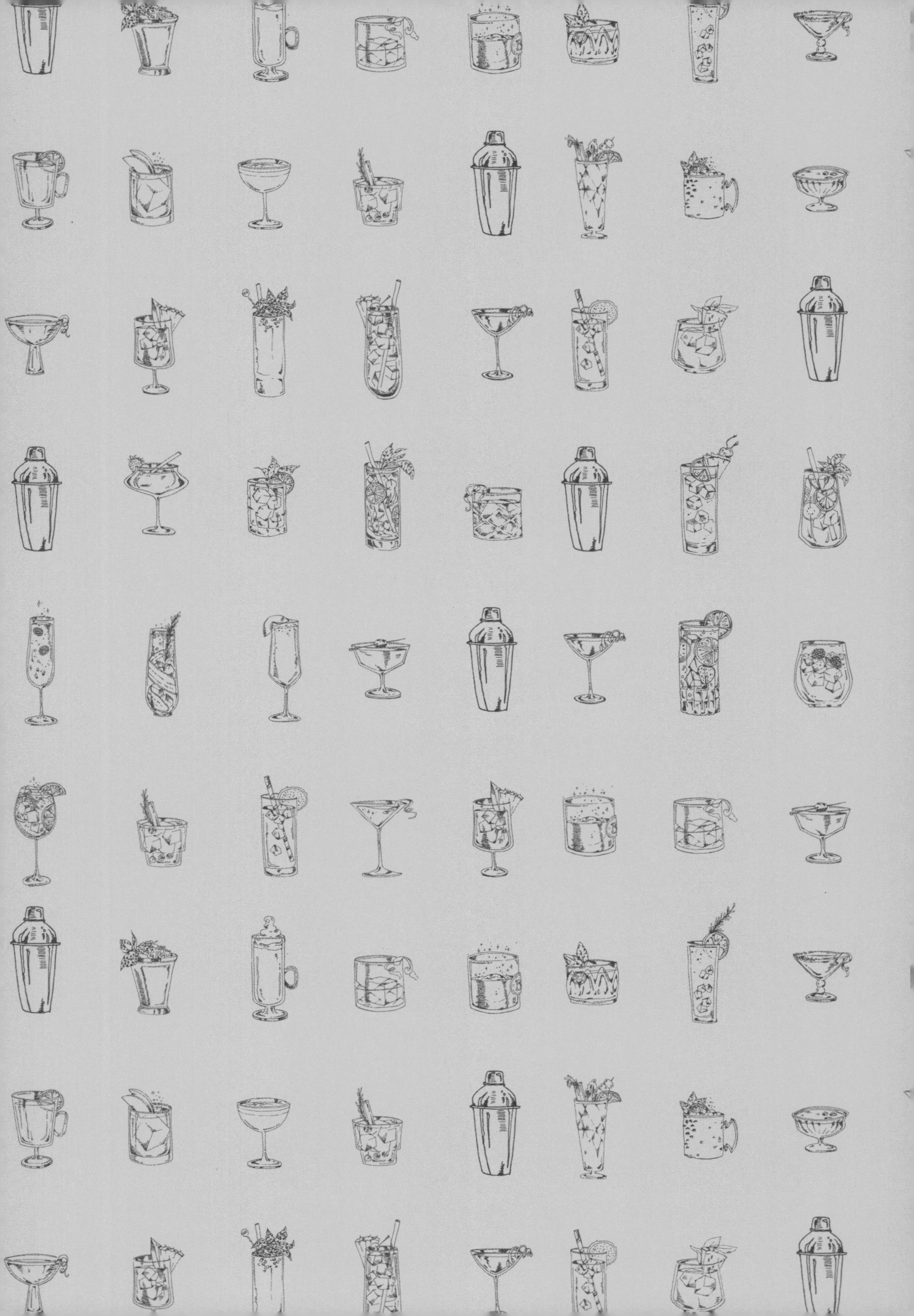

RUM

Rum is a spirit often associated with vacations and tropical climates. There's a reason for this: rum is distilled from molasses, which is created from sugarcane. Nearly all the sugarcane in the world is grown in balmy climates like Puerto Rico, Cuba, and the rest of the Caribbean. It only makes sense that places like these are where the Mojito, Mai Tai, and Piña Colada rose to prominence. Rum can come in a variety of styles, including white, amber, dark, spiced, and more. Like tequila, the darker the rum, the longer it's been aged in a barrel. The longer it ages, the richer and oakier the flavor. It's time to say "bon voyage" to all your troubles and take a tropical trip with me through this chapter!

LET'S MAKE THE:

Bluejay

SERVES: 2

GLASS: lowball

INGREDIENTS:

5 oz. Bacardi coconut rum
3 oz. cream of coconut
1.5 oz. blue Curaçao
2 oz. lime juice
0.25 tsp. almond extract
1 oz. simple syrup
mint sprigs
lime wheels

INSTRUCTIONS:

Combine all liquid ingredients in a shaker with ice and shake until well chilled. Strain into lowball glasses filled with small ice cubes. Slap your mint sprig on the back of your hand to release its scent, then add to each drink as a garnish along with the lime wheel.

NOTES:

This is my take on a Mai Tai, which is classified as a tiki drink. Tiki culture is inspired by the people and lifestyle of island people in the Pacific, including Polynesia and Hawaii. Most tiki drinks contain white or amber rum, fresh fruit juices, syrups, and spices like cinnamon or nutmeg. They famously come in rambunctious tiki mugs and almost always have a colorful umbrella added if you order them at a bar. If you're making them at home, choosing a fun glass and fresh fruit as your garnish will always do the trick.

LET'S MAKE THE:

Mojito

SERVES: 2

GLASS: Collins

INGREDIENTS:

4 oz. white rum
2 oz. lime juice
1 oz. simple syrup
club soda
mint leaves
lime wheels
cucumber slices

INSTRUCTIONS:

Add several mint leaves and simple syrup in the bottom of both glasses. Use a muddler to break down the leaves and release their scent. Fill each glass with small ice cubes and pour in your rum and lime juice. Stir gently before filling to the top with club soda. Insert cucumber slices and lime wheels around the walls of the glass and your final mint sprig on top.

NOTES:

The famous author Ernest Hemingway resided in Cuba and Key West at different times throughout the '40s and '50s and frequented local bars. He is said to have loved drinks like the Mojito, the Daiquiri, and many other rum- and gin-based cocktails. All of this is rumor, though, and probably just smart marketing. But the Mojito doesn't need advertising; anyone with two taste buds to rub together knows how good this cocktail can be when it's made well.

LET'S MAKE THE:

Classic Daiquiri

SERVES: 1

GLASS: martini

INGREDIENTS:

2 oz. white rum
2 oz. lime juice
0.5 oz. simple syrup
lime wheel

INSTRUCTIONS:

Combine all ingredients in a shaker with ice and shake until well chilled. Strain into a martini glass and add lime wheel for garnish.

NOTES:

The original Daiquiri was created in Havana, Cuba, sometime in the late 1890s. The drink is supposedly named after the mountain village town named Daiquiri. No wonder this beverage made its way down the mountaintop and into the world. With only three key ingredients, it remains an easy and delicious drink to make.

LET'S MAKE THE:

Frozen Daiquiri

SERVES: 8-10

GLASS: martini

INGREDIENTS:

10 oz. white rum
8-10 strawberries, frozen
juice of 5 limes
4 oz. simple syrup
0.5 cup of ice
lime wheels
strawberries

INSTRUCTIONS:

In a blender, combine all ingredients except for the garnishes. Blend until smooth. Distribute your frozen daiquiri mixture among all the glasses and skewer fresh strawberries and lime wheels to add as the finishing touch.

NOTES:

Constantino Ribalaigua Vert is the bartender credited with creating the first Frozen Daiquiri, which would become the most well-known form of a Daiquiri. Ribalaigua worked at the El Floridita bar, where Ernest Hemingway was a frequent customer, and is the reason why Hemingway loved rum so much.

LET'S MAKE THE:

Saint Simon

SERVES: 2

GLASS: lowball

INGREDIENTS:

4 oz. white rum
2 oz. pineapple juice
2 oz. cream of coconut
2 oz. lime juice
2 oz. orange juice
pineapple leaves & wedges

INSTRUCTIONS:

Combine all ingredients in a shaker with ice and shake until well chilled. Strain into two glasses filled with crushed ice. Garnish each with a pineapple wedge and leaf.

NOTES:

This refreshing, homemade version of a Piña Colada skips all the unnecessary syrupy sweetness. The essence of a good beach drink is to utilize the flavors local to that place; fresh coconut and pineapple juice beats store-bought syrups any day. I named this drink after Saint Simons Island, the beach my hubby and I visit most often.

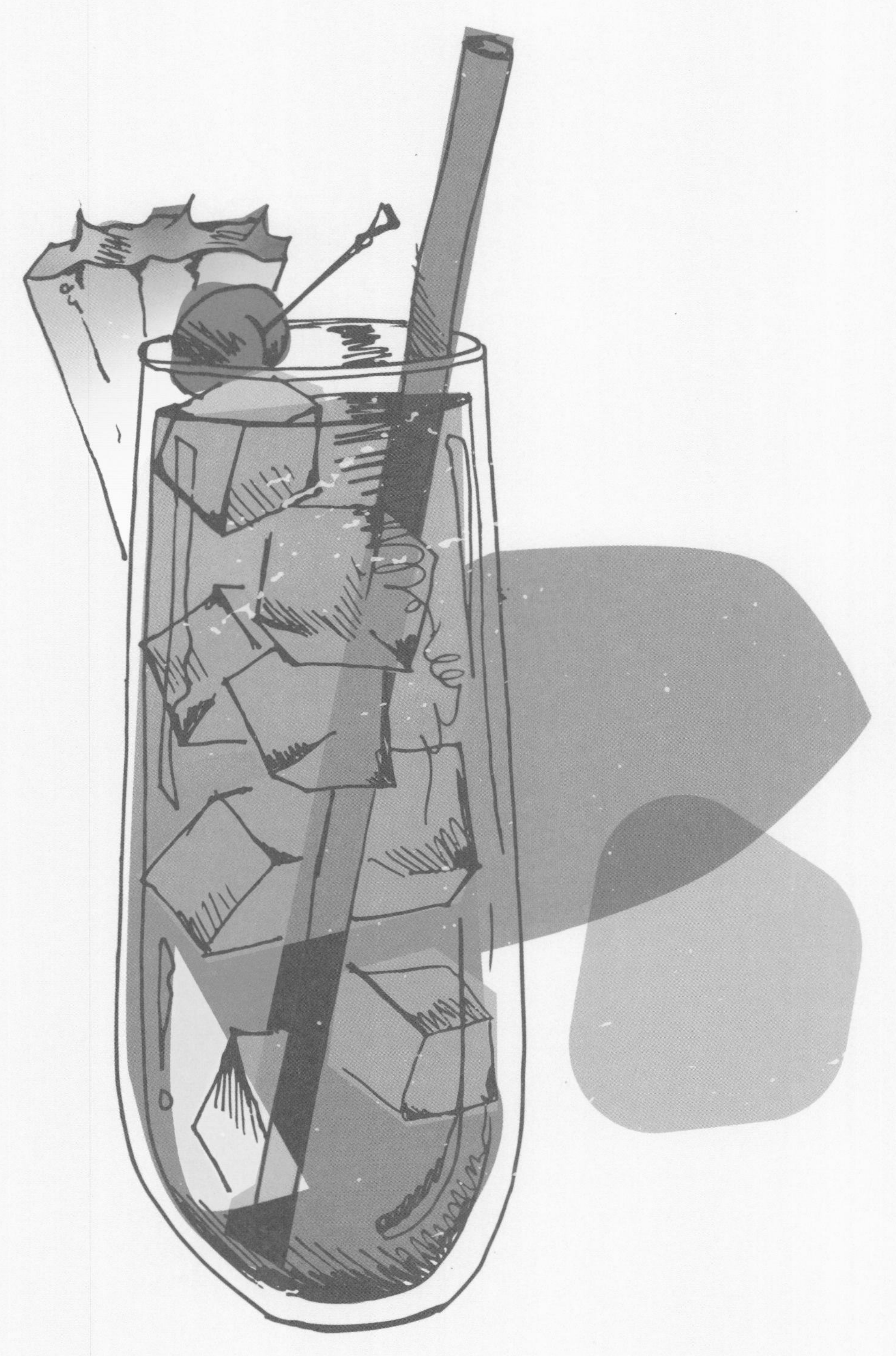

LET'S MAKE THE:

Bahama Mama

SERVES: 1

GLASS: Collins

INGREDIENTS:

1 oz. dark rum
1 oz. coconut rum
0.5 oz. Kahlúa
4 oz. pineapple juice
1 oz. fresh lemon juice
pineapple wedge
brandied cherry

INSTRUCTIONS:

Add all liquid ingredients to a shaker with ice and shake until well chilled. Fill a Collins glass with small ice cubes and strain your drink. Skewer a brandied cherry and pineapple wedge to add as the garnish.

NOTES:

You might have done a double-take on the ingredient list, but you read it right; a traditional Bahama Mama utilizes a coffee liqueur to counteract the sweetness of the fruit and rum. The result is a creamy, delicious beverage that is truly vacation-worthy.

CECE

LET'S MAKE THE:

Rum Swizzle

SERVES: 2

GLASS: Collins

INGREDIENTS:

4 oz. dark rum
1 oz. fresh lemon juice
1 oz. triple sec
ginger ale
lemon wheel
mint sprigs (optional)

INSTRUCTIONS:

Combine all ingredients except ginger ale and lemon wheel in a shaker with ice and shake until well chilled. Strain into two highball glasses filled with small ice cubes. Top both with ginger ale. Garnish each with a lemon wheel and optional mint sprigs.

NOTES:

This is the national cocktail of Bermuda, and the proper way to enjoy this drink is with a fancy swizzle stick or straw. Make sure to stir well before you sip, to adequately cool this drink down. You should enjoy your swizzle frosty cold.

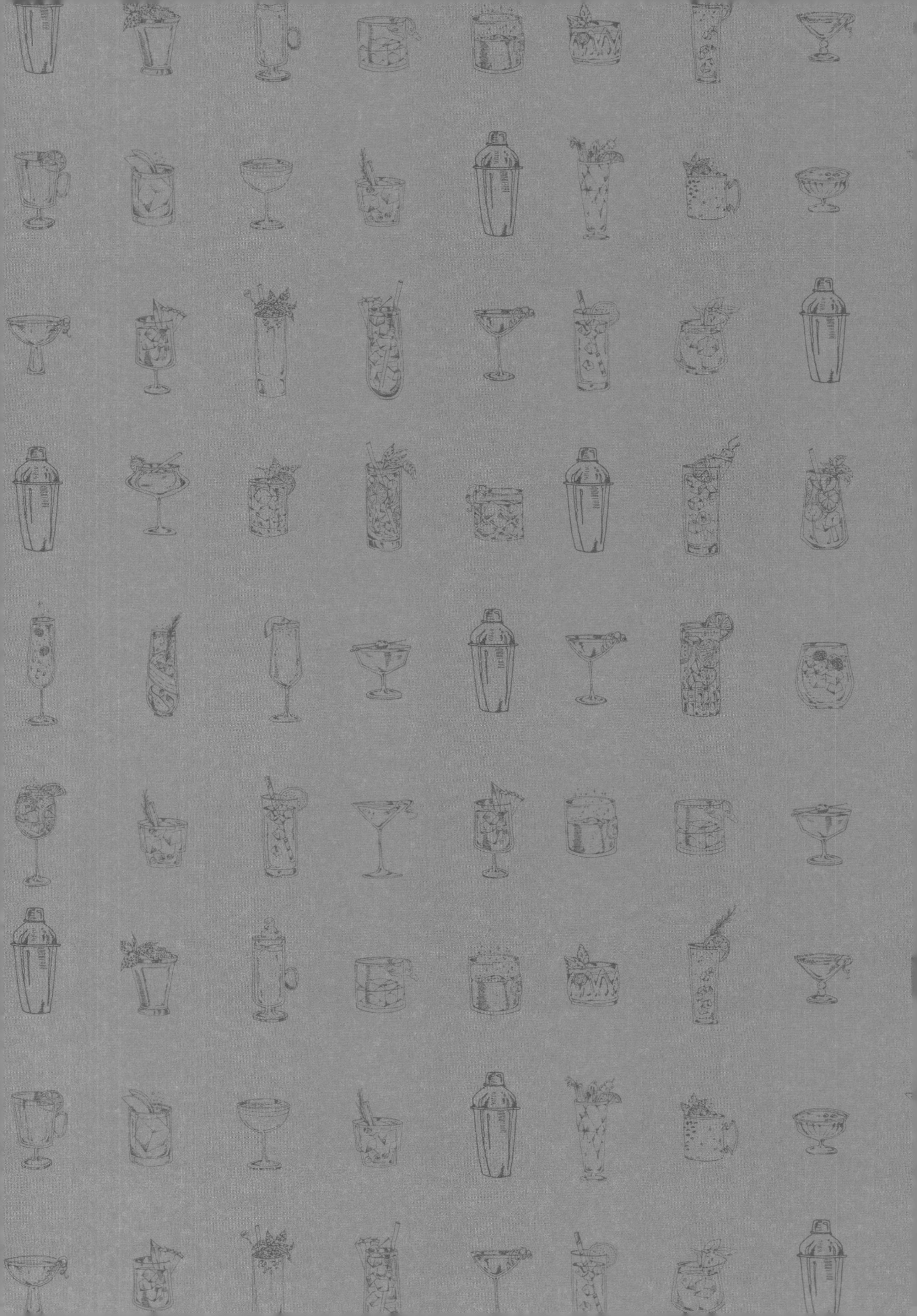

WHISKEY

The earliest documentation of whiskey production is from Ireland and Scotland in the 15th century. The early forms of this spirit were not aged in casks and, as a result, probably tasted horrific. But I suppose when you're living in the Middle Ages and just trying to catch a buzz, anything will do. Today, whiskey production is strictly regulated and has to meet many standards.

The distillation process utilizes a fermented grain mash that can include a variety of grains, including barley, corn, rye, and wheat. All whiskey, no matter the grain used, is aged in a barrel or cask and has a beautiful amber or chocolate hue by the end. There are many different kinds, including bourbons, rye whiskeys, scotches, and many others. Whiskeys have a particularly rich flavor and will be your drink's star. If you are a fan of whiskey's prominent flavor, you will have fun with this chapter.

LET'S MAKE THE:

Old Fashioned

SERVES: 1

GLASS: lowball

INGREDIENTS:

2 oz. bourbon or rye whiskey
a pinch of granulated sugar
Angostura bitters
0.5 tsp. warm water
orange peel

INSTRUCTIONS:

You will build this drink directly in the glass. Add sugar to the bottom of an empty glass and saturate with 3–4 drops of bitters and a splash of warm water to dissolve the sugar. Add a large ice cube. Pour in your bourbon or whiskey and stir gently to chill the drink. Express an orange peel over the glass and run along the rim before placing it in your drink as the garnish.

NOTES:

Originally dubbed "the Whiskey Cocktail" in the 1800s, this drink has long been considered a bar standard. As mixology evolved into newer and more complicated recipes, people began asking for an "old fashioned" drink, which quickly became its new namesake. It's a staple, especially in cold months; I like to make a holly-jolly version during the holidays by substituting the sugar with gingerbread syrup and garnishing with a gingerbread cookie.

B

LET'S MAKE THE:

Bailey Bullet

SERVES: 2

GLASS: lowball

INGREDIENTS:

4 oz. 1792 Kentucky Bourbon
Barq's root beer

INSTRUCTIONS:

In two cocktail glasses, place a large ice cube or ice sphere. Pour 2 oz. of 1792 Kentucky Bourbon in each. Fill to top with Barq's root beer.

NOTES:

This drink is my dad's concoction, and it deserved a spot in this book. If an Old Fashioned feels too heavy handed for you, try this instead. When both my dad and grandpa were pilots in the Marines, they used to fly a small, recreational, twin-engine plane back and forth between West Palm Beach and Boston. They deemed that machine the Bailey Bullet, and I deemed this sweet drink the same.

LET'S MAKE THE:

Whiskey Sour

SERVES: 2

GLASS: coupe

INGREDIENTS:

4 oz. bourbon or whiskey
2 oz. lemon juice
1 oz. simple syrup
1 egg white

INSTRUCTIONS:

Add your liquid ingredients to a shaker with ice and shake until well chilled. Strain into chilled coupe glasses. Add a few dashes of Angostura bitters on top of the froth of each drink.

NOTES:

Many folks make a popular alternative to this traditional recipe that skips the egg white and serves the drinks in a lowball glass over ice with a maraschino cherry as the garnish. I like both versions! The traditional is better suited for a high-end vibe with a fancy coupe glass. The quicker, eggless alternative is great for serving multiple people quickly. Two ways to make it means twice the fun.

LET'S MAKE THE:

Irish Coffee

SERVES:

2

GLASS:

Irish Coffee mug or tempered mug

INGREDIENTS:

3 oz. Irish whiskey
2 tsp. brown sugar
freshly brewed coffee
heavy cream
whipped cream

INSTRUCTIONS:

In each glass, pour 1.5 oz. of Irish whiskey. Add a tsp. of brown sugar to each. Fill nearly to the top with hot coffee, leaving room for cream. Add heavy cream to your liking and then top with whipped cream.

NOTES:

Coffee is a staple in my life, so it only makes sense that it's also in a cocktail I love. An Irish Coffee can be as extravagant as your decadent Starbucks order, so experiment with flavored syrups, spices, and whatever else gets your heart racing . . . you know, besides the caffeine.

LET'S MAKE THE:

Bourbon Smash

SERVES: 2

GLASS: lowball

INGREDIENTS:

0.5 cup frozen blueberries, slightly thawed
2 oz. lemon juice
1 oz. simple syrup
4 oz. bourbon
club soda
cinnamon sticks
rosemary sprigs
cinnamon

INSTRUCTIONS:

Divide your thawing blueberries between glasses. Add 1 oz. lemon juice, 0.5 oz. simple syrup, and a pinch of cinnamon to each glass. Muddle until you have a nice blueberry pulp. Add small ice cubes or crushed ice. Pour 2 oz. bourbon into each glass and top with club soda. Stir to mix drinks and chill. Garnish with fresh rosemary sprigs and cinnamon sticks.

NOTES:

Even if you don't consider yourself a dark liquor person, I dare you to try this one out; the rich, caramel flavors of bourbon combine so well with the blueberries and cinnamon to make an equally sweet and savory treat. You can also swap the fruit out for strawberries, blackberries, or raspberries—whatever floats your bourbon boat.

LET'S MAKE THE:

Mint Julep

SERVES:

2

GLASS:

lowball or copper mug

INGREDIENTS:

6-8 mint leaves
1 oz. simple syrup
5 oz. bourbon
Angostura bitters

INSTRUCTIONS:

Muddle the mint leaves with 0.5 oz. simple syrup in each glass to release their scent. Add 2.5 oz. bourbon to each and then top with crushed ice. Stir gently until the drink is frosty cold. Add ice to fill drink to rim and garnish with an additional mint sprig.

NOTES:

If you plan to host your own Derby Day party and want to save time with prep work, consider infusing your bourbon with mint the week before. Use a large jar or container that you can close tightly, and add 8-10 crushed sprigs of mint. Pour in your bourbon and seal tightly. Let it sit in a cool, shady spot in your house for 3-5 days, then move it to the fridge. From here, you can fill cups with crushed ice, add a splash of simple syrup, and pour in the minty bourbon. You'll be off to the races in no time, buddy.

LET'S MAKE THE:

Hot Toddy

SERVES:

2

GLASS:

Irish Coffee mug
or tempered mug

INGREDIENTS:

4 oz. whiskey
1 oz. lemon juice
2 oz. brown sugar
1 teaspoon maple syrup
boiling water
lemon slices

INSTRUCTIONS:

Bring water to a boil in a tea kettle. Add your fresh lemon juice, syrup, and sugar to each glass. Top each with 2 oz. of whiskey. Fill each to top with your hot water and stir to combine. Garnish with a lemon slice.

NOTES:

The Hot Toddy most likely originated in British-occupied India around the 1600s. The drink is defined as containing scotch whiskey, hot water, and various herbs. As its popularity spread into pubs across Britain and Scotland during the cold winters, patrons would often drink it out of a large, shared bowl (yeah, gross). Today, it's often served in a tempered glass mug, which is much more aesthetically and hygienically pleasing.

LET'S MAKE THE:

Poison Apple

SERVES: 2

GLASS: lowball

INGREDIENTS:

4 oz. bourbon
2 oz. apple cider vinegar
2 tsp. maple syrup
4 oz. pressed apple cider
ginger beer
apple slices
cinnamon
sugar

INSTRUCTIONS:

Rim both glasses with a cinnamon sugar mixture and place a large ice cube in each. Combine bourbon, ACV, maple syrup, and apple cider in a shaker. Add ice and shake until well chilled. Strain the mixture into each glass and top with ginger beer. Garnish each with 2–3 thin apple slices.

NOTES:

The wholesome combination of cinnamon and apple meets its match in this drink with the warm, tempting bourbon and maple syrup combination. The tension is cooled off with a little ginger beer, but don't get it twisted; this mouth-watering cocktail bites back. This is the drink recipe you break out to welcome the beginning of sweater weather and *Hocus Pocus* binges.

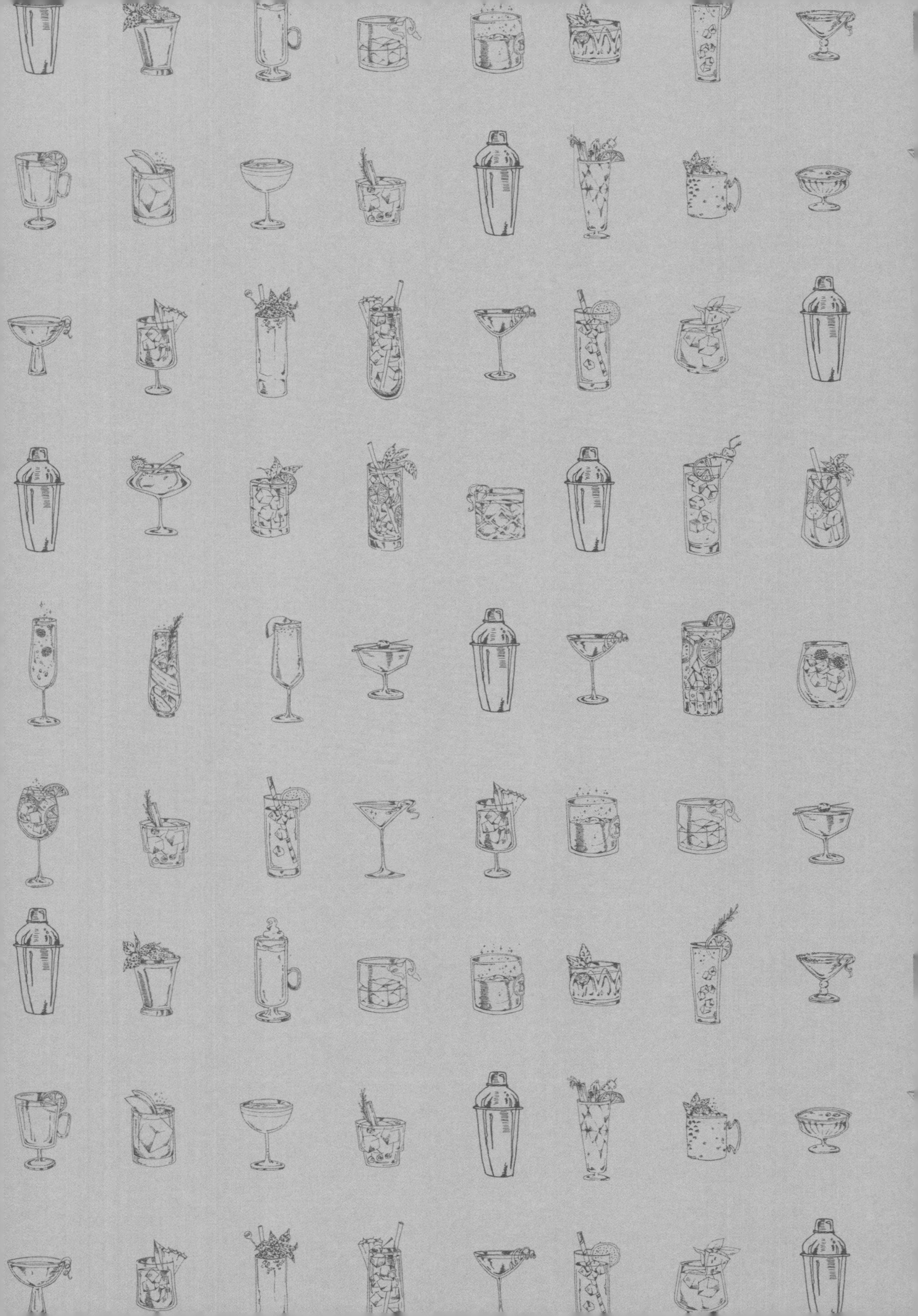

BUBBLY

When you picture a celebration in your mind, you probably envision glasses of glittery champagne. Every major life event features bubbly beverages, from weddings to baby showers to retirement parties to birthdays. Something about the sparkly nature of bubbles coincides with our happiest moments and shared celebrations.

Champagne is made from a very specific method native to France known as "the Classic Method." A still wine is created with fermented grapes, and then more sugars and yeast are added to the mixture to start a second fermentation process as it's bottled. The process in the bottle creates trapped carbon dioxide, producing the famous bubbly liquid. However, a bottle of this can be labeled "champagne" only if it's grown, fermented, and bottled in Champagne, France. If it's made anywhere else, it's simply known as sparkling wine. But "sparkling wine" simply does not have the same je ne sais quoi as "champagne," so call it whatever makes you feel fanciest.

Regardless, champagne is a wonderful addition on your bar cart, and there are plenty of fabulous ways to incorporate it into your cocktail menu at home.

LET'S MAKE THE:

New Year's Spritz

SERVES: 4

GLASS: flute

INGREDIENTS:

Angostura bitters
4 oz. grapefruit juice
champagne
pomegranate arils
raspberries

INSTRUCTIONS:

Add 2–3 dashes of bitters in each glass. Add 1 oz. of grapefruit juice to each glass and then fill it to the top with your favorite champagne. Drop 2–3 pomegranate arils into each glass and then float a few raspberries in each as garnish.

NOTES:

I originally made this for NYE one year; hence the name. But it's delicious for any time of the year and dresses up a simple glass of champagne. The garnish game is crucial when serving bubbly, so skip the midnight kiss and sip on this Insta-worthy spritz instead.

LET'S MAKE THE:

French 75

SERVES: 4

GLASS: flute

INGREDIENTS:

8 oz. gin
3 oz. lemon juice
2 oz. simple syrup
champagne
lemon peels

INSTRUCTIONS:

Combine gin, lemon juice, and simple syrup in a shaker with ice and shake until well chilled. Strain equally into your chilled flute glasses. Top each with champagne and garnish with lemon peel.

NOTES:

The French 75 is a brunch cocktail staple. To me, it's more balanced than a mimosa and the perfect drink to serve at a daytime gathering. I almost always make mine with Empress gin for a unique, lavender-hued drink.

LET'S MAKE THE:

Aperol Spritz

SERVES:

4

GLASS:

wine glass

INGREDIENTS:

8 oz. Aperol
12 oz. prosecco
club soda
orange slices

INSTRUCTIONS:

You will build this drink directly in the glass. Fill 4 wine glasses with small ice cubes. Add 2 oz. Aperol and 3 oz. prosecco to each glass and fill the rest of the way with club soda. Stir gently with your bar spoon to combine and chill. Insert 1–2 orange slices into each drink for garnish.

NOTES:

There's a common phrase in Italy: "Il dolce far niente." It translates to mean "the sweetness of doing nothing." Italians are very big on slowing down and enjoying time together. That's probably why this aperitivo (pre-dinner) drink is so popular there. It's the perfect beverage to make you sip, stay, and relax.

LET'S MAKE THE:

Sorrento Slice

SERVES:

4

GLASS:

wine glass

INGREDIENTS:

4 oz. vodka
8 oz. limoncello
2 oz. lemon juice
prosecco
lemon peels

INSTRUCTIONS:

You will build this drink directly in the glass. Fill 4 wine glasses with small ice cubes. Add 1 oz. vodka, 2 oz. limoncello, and 0.5 oz. lemon juice to each glass, then fill each to top with prosecco. Garnish with lemon peels.

NOTES:

While the Aperol Spritz gets a good amount of (well-deserved) attention, the real Italian superstar is limoncello, especially along the Amalfi Coast in places like Positano, Sorrento, and Capri. There are quite literally fresh lemons for sale everywhere you go. More than any other beverage, this drink reminds me of Italy and all the fresh tastes and smells the country has to offer.

LET'S MAKE THE:

Secret Garden

SERVES: 4

GLASS: flute

INGREDIENTS:

4 oz. vodka
4 oz. St. Germain
champagne
cucumber slices
rosemary sprigs

INSTRUCTIONS:

You will build this drink directly in the glass. In each flute, add a long slice of cucumber spiraled along the walls of the glass. Next, fill with small ice cubes. Add 1 oz. vodka and 1 oz. elderflower liqueur to each flute and then fill to top with champagne. Garnish with a fresh rosemary sprig.

NOTES:

I always keep St. Germain liqueur on hand in my fridge. It has a sweet, floral taste that mixes well with clear spirits like vodka and gin to make a refreshing beverage. It pairs well with any fruit or herb you want to add to a cocktail, so I highly recommend adding this as a trusty staple to your bar cart.

LET'S MAKE THE:

Peach Bellini

SERVES:

4

GLASS:

flute

INGREDIENTS:

8 oz. peach purée
prosecco
peach slices
lemon juice (optional)

INSTRUCTIONS:

Add 2 oz. of fresh peach purée to each champagne glass. Fill each to top with prosecco and gently stir with your bar spoon to combine purée and bubbly. Finish off each with a fresh peach slice for your garnish.

NOTES:

If you're like me and aren't crazy about supersweet drinks, add 0.5 oz. of lemon juice to each serving to balance out the flavors. Bada bing, bada Bellini.

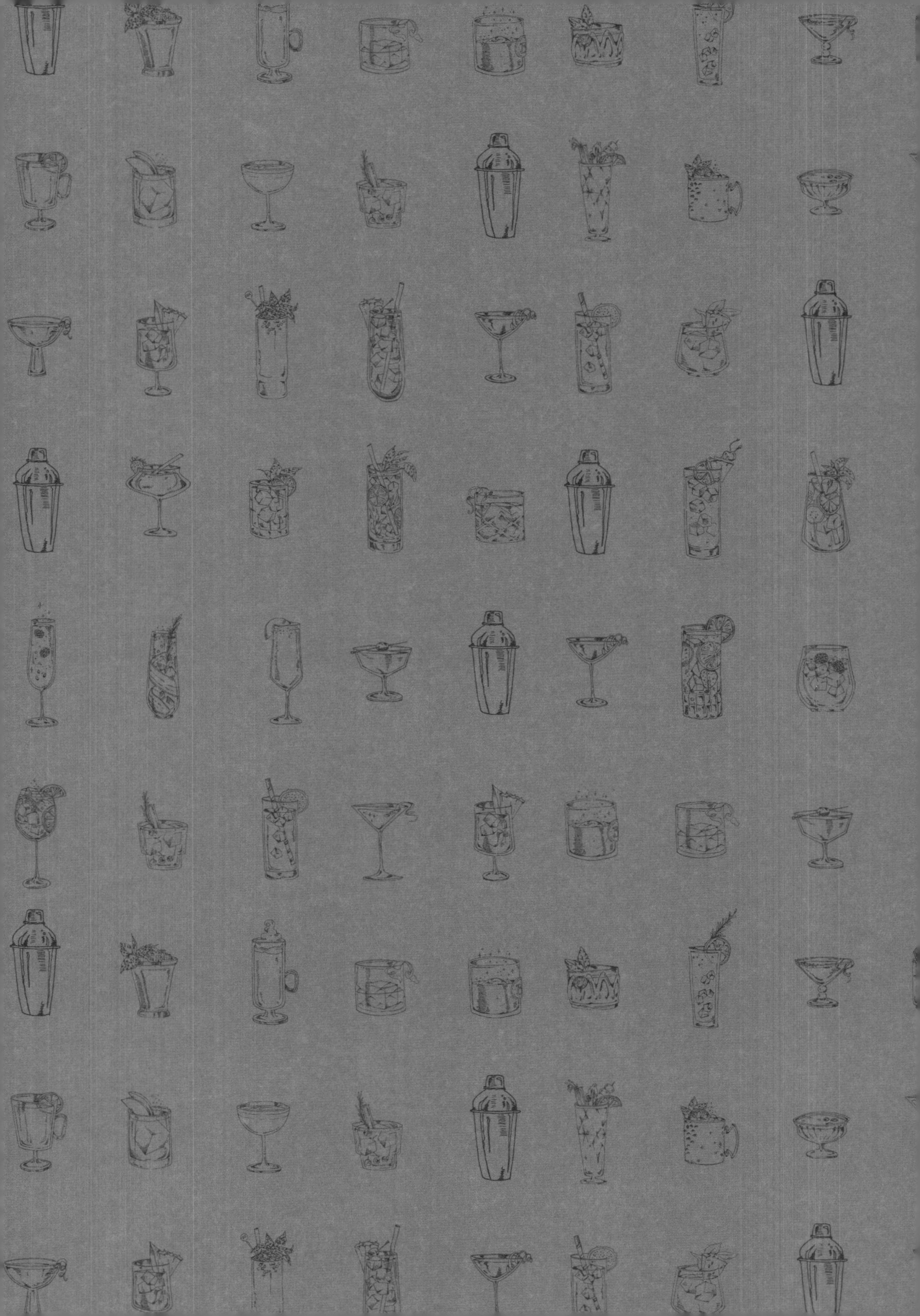

CLEAN

Not everyone drinks alcohol, but everyone deserves something to sip on while you're hosting them! I made this final chapter all about "clean cocktails," which contain no alcohol but are still just as refreshing and enjoyable as the drinks that preceded this page. Don't ever wait for people to ask for a nonalcoholic option or question why they're not drinking liquor. That's not your business, sweetheart!

If you're hosting a gathering, offer a clean beverage option right when guests arrive. Even if you don't have time to create a separate cocktail, you should always have tea, lemonade, or another alternative to plain water. If there's something my southern belle mother taught me well, it's that the best host is an inclusive host who welcomes everyone as they are. Cheers!

LET'S MAKE THE:

Companion

SERVES:

1

GLASS:

lowball

INGREDIENTS:

basil leaves
0.5 oz. lemon juice
0.5 oz. simple syrup
Topo Chico

INSTRUCTIONS:

You can build this drink directly in the glass. Add your simple syrup, lemon juice, and fresh basil leaves to a rocks glass. Muddle to release essence and then add several large ice cubes. Fill to top with Topo Chico. Add an additional basil leaf as your garnish.

NOTES:

I named this drink the Companion because it is the best sidekick to whatever you're doing. Cooking, reading, knitting, unicycling, lounging, gardening, etc. It goes well with everything. Actually, I advise you not to drink this and ride a unicycle; it's nonalcoholic, but you may spill, and that's not fun for anyone.

LET'S MAKE THE:

Fragaria Fresca

SERVES: 1

GLASS: Collins

INGREDIENTS:

2 oz. DHOS nonalcoholic gin
1 oz. strawberry simple syrup
0.5 oz. lime juice
Sprite
fresh strawberries
rosemary sprig

INSTRUCTIONS:

In a highball glass, muddle a few strawberries and then fill with ice. Add 2 oz. DHOS nonalcoholic gin, 1 oz. strawberry simple syrup, and 0.5 oz. lime juice to your glass. Fill to the top with Sprite. Garnish with a fresh strawberry and rosemary sprig.

NOTES:

There are tons of great options for nonalcoholic spirits. Some of my favorites include Seedlip, DHOS, and Lyre's. Experiment with them to figure out what flavors work best with the drinks you like to make, and add them as a regular staple to your bar cart.

LET'S MAKE THE:

Piña Buck

SERVES: 1

GLASS: copper mug

INGREDIENTS:

2 oz. pineapple juice
chopped jalapeño
0.5 lime juice
ginger beer
mint leaves

INSTRUCTIONS:

Fill a copper mug with ice. In a shaker, combine fresh pineapple juice, chopped jalapeño slices, and lime juice with ice and shake until well chilled. Strain into a mug and fill to the top with ginger beer. Garnish with a fresh sprig of mint.

NOTES:

If you want an extra spicy version of this, mix up your pineapple juice, lime juice, and jalapeños a few hours ahead of time and let the mixture sit in the fridge. The peppers' spice will fully soak in and produce a buck with plenty of kick. Buck me up, bro.

LET'S MAKE THE:

Shirley Temple

SERVES: 1

GLASS: Collins

INGREDIENTS:

1 oz. grenadine
ginger ale
maraschino cherries

INSTRUCTIONS:

Fill a Collins glass with ice. Add 1 oz. of grenadine. Fill to the top with ginger ale and garnish with several maraschino cherries.

NOTES:

It's almost a requirement to include a fun straw when you serve this drink, so the person enjoying it can swirl the grenadine, cherries, and ginger ale around as they sip. It's always fun to feel fancy!

LET'S MAKE THE:

Zombie Zinger

SERVES: 1

GLASS: lowball

INGREDIENTS:

2 oz. cranberry juice
1 oz. orange juice
2 oz. lemonade
orange wheel

INSTRUCTIONS:

Fill a rocks glass with a few large ice cubes. Combine all liquid ingredients with ice in a shaker and shake until well chilled. Strain into your glass and garnish with an orange wheel.

NOTES:

I recommend chilling your glass in the freezer beforehand to enjoy this one fully. The tartness of cranberry juice tastes best to me when it's ice cold.

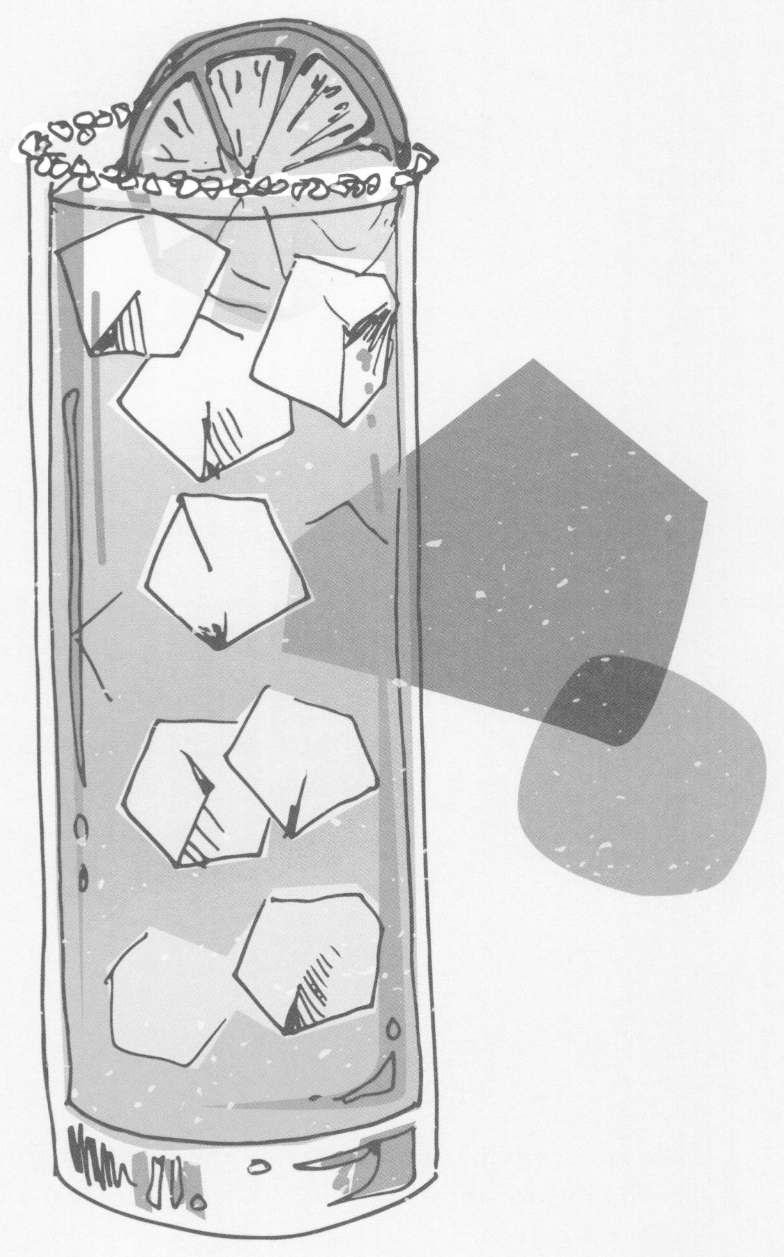

LET'S MAKE THE:

Elle Woods

SERVES: 1

GLASS: Collins

INGREDIENTS:

1 oz. grapefruit juice
0.5 oz. grenadine
0.5 oz. lime juice
Topo Chico
lime wheel
margarita salt

INSTRUCTIONS:

Rim a Collins glass with salt. Add the first three ingredients to a shaker with ice and shake until well chilled. Strain into the highball glass filled with ice and fill to top with Topo Chico. Garnish with a lime wheel.

NOTES:

This drink will have you doing the "bend and snap" in no time. Or studying for the bar. It depends on what type of person you are. Or if you're like Elle, you can be brainy and bubbly at the same time. "What, like it's hard?"

LET'S MAKE THE:

Firecracker

SERVES: 1

GLASS: Collins

INGREDIENTS:

2 oz. apple cider vinegar
1 oz. lemon juice
0.5 oz. simple syrup
cayenne pepper
club soda
lemon peel

INSTRUCTIONS:

You can build this drink directly in the glass. Fill your Collins glass with small ice cubes. Next, add the ACV, lemon juice, simple syrup, and cayenne pepper. Gently stir with your bar spoon before filling the rest with club soda. Garnish with a lemon peel.

NOTES:

ACV has many positive qualities but adds a tangy flavor to your drink, and that's why I like it. You can add a tablespoon to your water every morning to help your body expel toxins, promote good digestion, and improve circulation. Or, you could enjoy it in a sweet and spicy mocktail. Your choice.

LET'S MAKE THE:

Blue Pill

SERVES: 1

GLASS: lowball

INGREDIENTS:

blueberries
0.5 oz. lime juice
gingerberry kombucha
mint sprigs

INSTRUCTIONS:

Add blueberries and lime juice to a rocks glass and muddle until you have a nice pulp. Fill the glass halfway with ice and fill to top with gingerberry kombucha or kombucha flavor of your choice. Stir to combine, and add a mint sprig as garnish.

NOTES:

Kombucha is packed with health benefits, tastes amazing, and is a great substitute for a cocktail. You can swap around the fruits and kombucha flavor to your liking. Happy boochin'!

(C)ECE
PAGE

Cece Bailey Page is the author and illustrator of *The Bar(c)art Book*. She lives in Atlanta, Georgia, with her husband and two pups.

Cece is a full-time graphic designer and artist who enjoys bringing creative ideas to life for her clients.

You can reach out to her directly at the-cece-shop.com

DRINK LIST